POLICE LINE DO NOT CROSS

WHO WORKS IN MY NEIGHBORHOOD

THE POLICE OFFICER

Jared Siemens

LIGHTBOX
openlightbox.com

LIGHTBOX

Go to **www.openlightbox.com** and enter this book's unique code.

ACCESS CODE

LBXH4552

Lightbox is an all-inclusive digital solution for the teaching and learning of curriculum topics in an original, groundbreaking way. Lightbox is based on National Curriculum Standards.

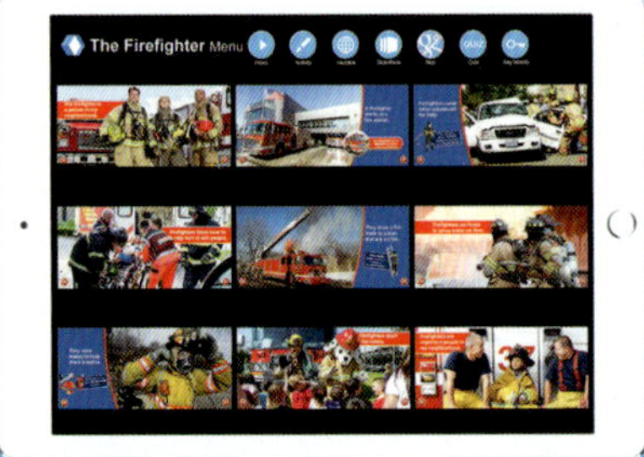

OPTIMIZED FOR

- ✓ **TABLETS**
- ✓ **WHITEBOARDS**
- ✓ **COMPUTERS**
- ✓ **AND MUCH MORE!**

STANDARD FEATURES OF LIGHTBOX

 **AUDIO** High-quality narration using text-to-speech system

 **VIDEOS** Embedded high-definition video clips

 **ACTIVITIES** Printable PDFs that can be emailed and graded

 **WEBLINKS** Curated links to external, child-safe resources

 **SLIDESHOWS** Pictorial overviews of key concepts

 **INTERACTIVE MAPS** Interactive maps and aerial satellite imagery

 **QUIZZES** Ten multiple choice questions that are automatically graded and emailed for teacher assessment

 **KEY WORDS** Matching key concepts to their definitions

VIDEOS

WEBLINKS

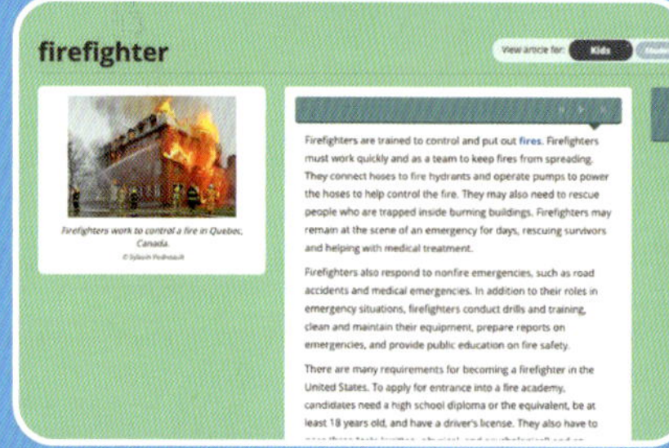

SLIDESHOWS

QUIZZES

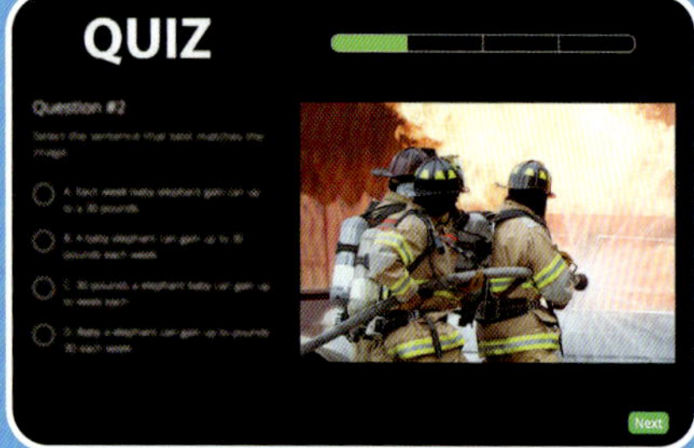

THE POLICE OFFICER

Contents

POLICE DEPARTMENT
METRO
BRADLEY
4

The police officer is a person in my neighborhood.

CITY OF PORTLAND
POLICE BUREAU
NO SMOKING
IN THIS AREA
PORTLAND POLICE
Sworn to Protect
Dedicated to Serve
POLICE
6

A police officer works at a police station.

The **New York City Police Department** is the **largest** police department in the **United States.**

The police officer keeps people safe and makes sure they follow the rules.

There are about **15,400** police departments across the **United States**.

SHERIFF
DEPT

Police officers get called when people have car accidents.

12

Police dogs help police officers do their jobs.

Police dogs were **first used** in the United States in **1907**.

A police officer looks for people who are lost.

The police officer stops people who are driving too fast and tells them to slow down.

POLICE
PROTECT
SERVE
OFFICIAL
COURT

The police officer teaches me about rules and safety.

He tells me to call 911 if someone is in danger.

Police officers are important people in my neighborhood.

See what you have learned about the police officer.

Describe what you see in each of the pictures.

KEY WORDS

Research has shown that as much as 65 percent of all written material published in English is made up of 300 words. These 300 words cannot be taught using pictures or learned by sounding them out. They must be recognized by sight. This book contains 43 common sight words to help young readers improve their reading fluency and comprehension. This book also teaches young readers several important content words, such as proper nouns. These words are paired with pictures to aid in learning and improve understanding.

Page	Sight Words First Appearance
5	a, in, is, my, the
7	at, city, new, states, works
8	about, and, are, follow, keeps, makes, people, there, they
11	car, get, have, when
13	do, first, help, their, used, were
14	for, looks, who
16	down, stops, tells, them, to, too
18	me
19	call, he, if
21	important

Page	Content Words First Appearance
5	neighborhood, person, police officer
7	New York City Police Department, police department, station, United States
8	rules
11	accidents
13	jobs, police dogs
14	lost
18	safety
19	danger

Published by Smartbook Media Inc.
350 5th Avenue, 59th Floor, New York, NY 10118
Website: www.openlightbox.com

Library of Congress Control Number: 2020934521

ISBN 978-1-5105-5357-6 (hardcover)
ISBN 978-1-5105-5358-3 (multi-user eBook)

Printed in Guangzhou, China
1 2 3 4 5 6 7 8 9 0 24 23 22 21 20

042020
110819

Project Coordinator: Ryan Smith
Designer: Ana María Vidal

The publisher acknowledges Getty Images, iStock, and Shutterstock as the primary image suppliers for this title.